THIS BOOK BELONGS TO:

____

Celebrate & Learn!
Series
Independence Day
Freedom, Fireworks,
and American History

Dedicated to all who love to learn.

ISBN 978-1-970416-04-6

www.joeysavestheday.com

Mimi Books™ Publishing

A Mimi Book

Independence Day is celebrated every year on July 4th.

IN CONGRESS, JULY 4, 1776.

The unanimous Declaration of the thirteen united States of America.

It marks the day the Declaration of Independence was approved in 1776.

The Declaration said the American colonies were free from Great Britain.

FREEDOM

Thomas Jefferson wrote most of the Declaration.

JEFFERSON

The Declaration was signed in Philadelphia, Pennsylvania.

John Hancock signed his name the biggest so the king could "read it without his glasses."

Pennsylvania

The building where it was signed is called Independence Hall.

The Declaration of Independence has 1,458 words.

The first Independence Day celebration happened in 1777, one year later.

The Liberty Bell in Philadelphia is a famous symbol of freedom.

The Liberty Bell is known for its famous crack.

FIREWORKS

Fireworks have been part of July 4th since 1777. Americans use more than 200 million pounds of fireworks each year.

Many cities hold big fireworks shows, like New York, Boston, and Washington, D.C.

Sparklers burn at over 1,000°F, so they must be used safely.

Parades are a popular way to celebrate the holiday.

Some families celebrate with backyard barbecues. Red, white, and blue decorations fill homes and neighborhoods.

4th of July

Many families celebrate with hot dogs, hamburgers, and corn on the cob. Americans eat about 150 million hot dogs on July 4th.

Watermelon is one of the most popular July 4th treats.

The American flag has 13 stripes for the original colonies.

50
It has 50 stars for the 50 states.
4th of JULY

The colors red, white, and blue
stand for valor, purity, and justice.

The bald eagle became the national bird in 1782.

The National Bird

The Statue of Liberty is a symbol of freedom and friendship.

Freedom & Friendship

Patriotic songs like "America the Beautiful" are often sung on July 4th.
4TH
— OF —
JULY

The national motto is "In God We Trust."

The Great Seal of the United States shows an eagle holding arrows and an olive branch.
SEAL OF THE PRESIDENT OF THE UNITED STATES
E PLURIBUS UNUM

About 2.5 million people lived in the colonies in 1776.

Today, more than 330 million people live in the United States.

1776

Thomas Jefferson and John Adams both died on July 4, 1826, exactly 50 years later.

John Adams

The second President of the United States.

Thomas Jefferson

The third President of the United States.

Calvin Coolidge is the only U.S. president born on July 4th.

4th of July

30th President

Independence Day celebrates the idea that people should have rights and freedoms.

The Declaration says all people are created equal. It also says people have the right to life, liberty, and the pursuit of happiness.

LIFE
LIBERTY
AND THE
PURSUIT OF HAPPINESS

LISTEN
The Founding Fathers wanted a government that listened to the people.

BE THANKFUL FOR FREEDOMS

The holiday reminds us to be thankful for our freedoms.

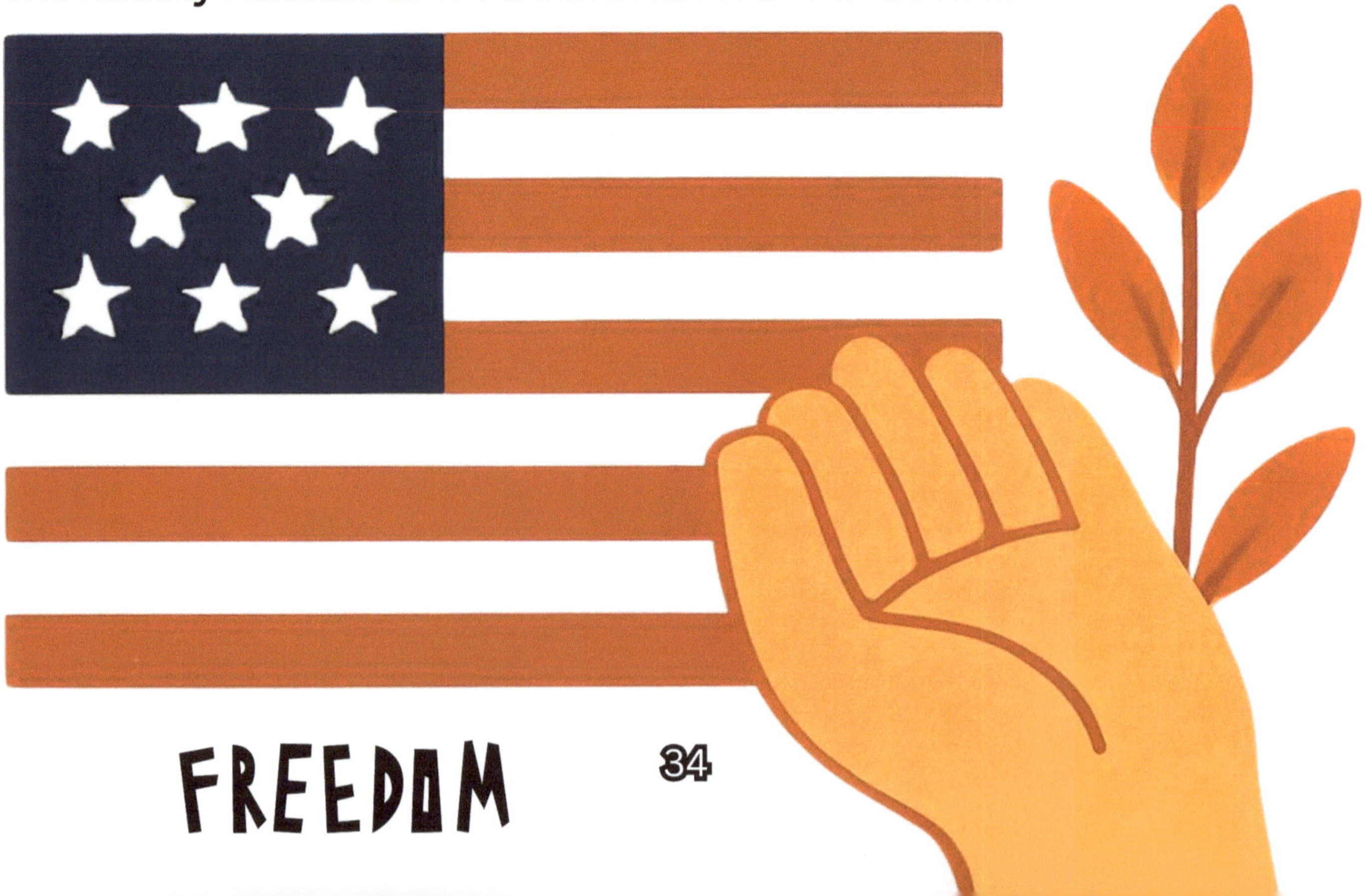

The U.S. Constitution was written 11 years after the Declaration.

Independence Day is a time to celebrate unity, freedom, and the American spirit.

UNITY

FREEDOM AND THE AMERICAN SPIRIT

Thank you for celebrating and learning with me today. I hope you discovered something new and had fun exploring this special holiday together.

If you enjoyed this book, please consider leaving a review. It helps other families discover it too.

See you in the next celebration!

www.ingramcontent.com/pod-product-compliance
Lightning Source LLC
LaVergne TN
LVHW070159110826
845147LV00002B/449

9781970416046